Dear Black Nation

Emick Lee

I0459252

DEAR BLACK NATION

EMICK LEE

Copyright

Published by Emick Lee Publishing

For permission to use material from this book, please contact: emicklee@myyahoo.com

Paperback

ISBN: 978-1-967385-04-1

Ebook

ISBN: 978-1-967385-06-5

Printed in the United States

Editorial direction & production by **Antonio T. Smith Sr. Ministries**

First Edition: 2025

Author's Note

Dear Brother Smith,

Thank you. For your time, your steadiness, your eye that sees seed inside soil. These pages are rough yet legible, tender yet true; please move with patience toward clarity, as you always do. I'm grateful your hands—and spirit—are upon this work.

Thank you for treating every margin note like a compass and every edit like gentle rain. Your care reminds me that books are midwifed, not manufactured. Where my words are tangled, help me untie them; where the voice quivers, help me breathe; where the truth is brightest, help me polish without dimming it.

I offer this manuscript with open palms: keep the soul intact as you refine the sentence; keep the heartbeat audible as you shape the frame. If any line lacks love, let us revise it. If any page lacks purpose, let us repurpose it. Our aim is service—to God, to our people, to anyone who needs a lantern in a long night.

Thank you for honoring the ancestors in the cadence, the children in the promise, and the present in the courage it takes to speak. May every correction be a kindness, every suggestion a prayer, and every improvement a small act of healing. I bless your eyes, your hours, and your craft.

With gratitude that overflows and love that endures, I entrust this work to your care. May it rise better than it arrived, and may it travel farther than we imagined.

With love and deep thanks,

Emick Lee

Invocation to the Nation

Dear Black Nation, let us pray:

May God's universal peace be extended through me to you.

May His knowledge take root and grow.

May we become the foundation the Creator sets forth.

May we turn to the All-Knowing and wise.

May we stop being wise in our own eyes.

May we give back to other nations their lies.

May we become our brothers' and sisters' keepers—instead of suppliers, plugs, murderers, recruiters, or the architects of our own genocide.

May our "keep it real" become "keep it healed."

May gangsta rap die so the party does not die with the sound of the Glock.

May we speak our doubts and fears openly to one another.

May we respect our fathers and honor our mothers.

May we accept that we cannot love another until we love ourselves first.

May we remember that self-love is not hate.

May we love Black women and Black children—and let our gifts pour upon them like rain.

May laughter return where alcohol and drugs pretended to heal.

May we hold our heads high as we stand in front of our trials,

and walk out of them together—steadfast, whole, and free.

Foreword

Some books are written in comfort. This one was forged in confinement.

Emick Lee wrote these pages from inside a prison. He is incarcerated, but he is not a prisoner—neither in mind nor in action. From a place designed to subtract time, he has multiplied meaning. From a system built to mute, he has amplified a people's song. The walls around him do not define him; they frame a viewpoint the world needs: clarity from the belly of the machine, hope authored under pressure, freedom practiced where freedom is rationed.

This book is both prayer and plan, both altar call and architectural drawing. It is covenant text—line by line, vow by vow—summoning us from performance to purpose. Emick does not write as a spectator to suffering; he writes as a witness from within. That vantage makes the pages heavier—and holier.

I have watched Emick labor in the currency that cannot be counterfeited: love, discipline, and truth. The cadence is ancestral, the counsel practical, the courage contagious.

These chapters move us from "Amen" to assignment, from grief to governance, from feelings to frameworks. They insist that faith without works is dead—and then they hand you the works.

This book advances three moves we desperately need:

1) Spiritual reformation from the inside out. From a cell, Emick calls us back to the living Christ—away from cosmetic religion and toward fruit that feeds families, schools, and streets. He names idols, refuses excuses, and reopens the ancient path: repent, repair, rebuild. The invitation is not to become perfect overnight; it is to become led.

2) Nation-building as a daily discipline. These pages read like a kitchen-table constitution: honor mothers and fathers; defend women and children; apprentice the young; circulate economics like living water; turn sanctuaries into training grounds; keep books open, titles humble, power accountable. Budgets and calendars become spiritual documents. Wealth is recast as the ability to make others whole.

3) A homecoming for the diaspora—without permission slips. The text refuses smallness and dependency. It asks us to remember who we were before paperwork and to love each other across oceans without empire's approval. It summons us to trade dependence for alliance, spectacle for service, fragmentation for one drum—discipline at dawn, diligence at noon, devotion at night.

How should you read this? Out loud. In circles. In living rooms, classrooms, church basements, barber shops, boardrooms, reentry homes, and yes—inside facilities where hope is too often contraband. Read a page, then do a thing. Read another page, then build a team. Stack faithful days: literacy, sobriety, savings, therapy, worship, rest. Let the slow miracles add up.

Expect conviction. Expect hope. Expect the elders at your back and the children at your front. Expect clear lines about what must end and courageous steps toward what must begin. Expect receipts—visible outcomes, not merely visible opinions.

To Emick: thank you for proving that iron bars cannot cage a faithful pen. You have braided lament and logistics, prophecy and plan. You have practiced freedom where it is least expected and taught us how to do the same.

To you, the reader: consider yourself deputized. This is not content; it is covenant. Sign it with the way you live. Pray it at dawn, practice it by noon, protect it at dusk. And when you tire, rest without guilt—then rise and resume with joy. If you fall, stand with help. If you wander, let the covenant call you home.

We begin now.

And we do not stop.

With respect and resolve,

Antonio T. Smith Jr.

Density6 | Quantum AI | Quantum Encryption | Decentralized Infrastructure | Transparent Solar | Quantum Dot Tech | Genomic Medicine | Nano Tech | Robotics

The Covenant of One– Chapter 1

Let us pray: May God's universal peace be extended through me to you.

May we travel with knowledge, faith, truth, and growth.

May we see and come to the foundation of unity, speaking the Creator's truth.

May we attune to God and all in our community.

May we stop being wise only in our own eyes.

May we give back to other nations a part of their wealth.

May we become our brothers' and sisters' keepers instead of murderers, thieves, rapists, or oppressors.

May we reconnect and heal the wounds of our nation's genocide.

May our keen watch recall history and awaken us.

By choice, by insight, may we be lifted to the sound of the Creator.

May we stop the oppression of our own people and extend charity to one another.

May we teach our children to respect our fathers and honor our mothers.

From this, may we conclude:

We cannot truly love one another until we love ourselves first.

Then we will tolerate no self-hate in our midst.

God's will is that we live as one people.

May we unite Black nations everywhere.

May our light shine again to them.

Our souls are routing a path — may we walk it instead of wandering astray.

May we heal our wounds and lift our heads as we stand in the presence of great trials.

Let God wash away our shame.

May we overcome the chains of slavery once and for all.

Leaders, today see yourselves as leaders going forward — instead of mere workers and laborers for another's gain.

May we live for one another.

May we come to the earth's conclusion knowing God's will is for us to be whole.

Finally, may we speak words that raise our people and become the light for others.

May we travel together in unity.

May this prayer take wings and become a beacon around the world, one consciousness.

May we leave behind false gods.

May we make new worlds marked by true faith and righteous living.

Amen.

Now...

Let us rise from Amen and make it flesh.

May our yes become action.

May our hands remember the promise our mouths just made.

May our footsteps map the road our souls already know.

May we sanctify our mornings with purpose.

May our evenings account for the work done in love.

May our midnights keep vigil for the suffering, the lost, and the unheard.

May we build houses of learning where truth is not punished.

May we teach history without erasing our names.

May we restore languages, songs, and rhythms carried across waters and deserts.

May we turn our neighborhoods into sanctuaries.

May every porch be a watchtower of care.

May every kitchen table become a council for peace.

May every classroom become a forge for genius.

May we defend our women and protect our children.

May we honor our elders and provision our widows.

May we make room for the differently abled, the grieving, and the returning citizen.

May we lift those who fell to systems designed to trap them.

May we break every covenant with despair.

May we refuse any lie that calls us less than holy.

May we uproot bitterness and sow forgiveness with boundaries.

May we turn from vengeance and choose justice with wisdom.

May we keep our money moving like living water.

May we shop with each other, hire each other, insure each other, heal each other.

May we learn the disciplines of land, law, credit, and craft.

May we tithe to the future with scholarships, clinics, gardens, and studios.

May we be unbribed by fame and unmoved by flattery.

May we speak with the courage of prophets and the calm of builders.

May we organize without spectacle and win without needing applause.

May our art carry medicine.

May our sermons carry instruction.

May our politics carry compassion.

May our science carry humility.

May our businesses carry covenant.

May we set a watch over our tongues.

May we trade gossip for intercession.

May we trade envy for mentorship.

May we trade cynicism for plans and teams.

May the scattered return and the divided reconcile.

May the continent and the diaspora eat at one table.

May passports not separate what ancestry already joined.

May we bless nations that blessed us and forgive those that did not.

May we marry purpose to patience.

May we keep promises when the cameras leave.

May we stay faithful to the slow miracles–literacy, sobriety, savings, therapy, prayer.

May we rebuild what our grandparents dreamed and our parents could not finish.

May we bless their names and complete their assignments.

May we redeem lost time with disciplined years.

Leaders, take inventory:

May your authority be service.

May your counsel be clean.

May your circle be accountable.

May your power be transparent and your books be open.

Workers, take heart:

May your labor be dignified.

May your wages be fair.

May your breaks be real.

May your future be possible.

Artists, take aim:

May your craft uplift without lying.

May your stage be a pulpit of light.

May your pen be a plow.

May your lens be a window, not a mirror only.

Teachers, take courage:

May you teach to liberate, not just to test.

May you see the genius before the grade.

May you call the student by the name destiny knows.

Healers, take care:

May your hands remember Eden.

May your clinics become triage for the spirit and the body.

May your prescriptions include food, movement, and hope.

Saints, keep praying:

May your knees till the soil for our harvest.

May your faith be the roof we build beneath.

May your fasting become bread for those who hunger.

And when we are tired:

May rest visit us without guilt.

May Sabbath return to our calendars.

May laughter come back to our tables.

May music reopen our lungs.

From this day:

We renounce smallness.

We reject borrowed shame.

We refuse to be weaponized against one another.

From this day:

We draft family constitutions.

We write wills and fund trusts.

We insure our lives and our visions.

We buy land and keep it.

From this day:

We mentor two as we climb one rung.

We forgive wisely, reconcile safely, and protect fiercely.

We love out loud and correct in private.

If we wander, may the covenant call us home.

If we forget, may the children remind us.

If we fall, may we rise together and not alone.

Let the Creator witness this vow:

That our unity will not be theory,

That our mercy will not be rare,

That our excellence will not be accident.

May the next generation inherit more than our pain:

May they inherit systems that work,

Libraries that are full,

Accounts that are funded,

Passports that open doors,

Faith that travels,

And names that open gates.

So let the Amen become assignment.

So let the prayer become policy.

So let the vision become neighborhood.

We begin now.

And we do not stop.

Sovereign Wealth of the Spirit– Chapter 2

Understand that wealth is subjective and measured by one's ability to effect change.

May we never look for our value as human beings through material gains.

May we take with us the knowledge that we're spiritual creation, living in a world that has physical laws and principles.

May we stop the trend of being consumers.

May we find joy in doing for one another.

May we fall in love with our God of creation.

May we realize that earth and its resources are no one's property, and earth is not our final home.

May our spirit awaken, allowing us to receive our blessings.

May we find love, joy, and peace in the form of good deeds first.

May we stop living for gains against the truth of a thing.

If it hurts, may we find value within taking our time.

May we live with integrity the rest of our days.

May we come to peace with the messes we've made.

May we learn to trust in the voice of the Lord over the voice of man.

May the spirit of our ancestors now reach us.

May we receive the offering of the Lord Jesus Christ the Father has sent.

May we awaken out of the sleep cast upon us by the spirit of the American dream.

May we find and reunite with our brothers and sisters around the world.

May God restore our birthright as a chosen people upon the nations.

May the true man and woman of God please stand up.

May we now walk within the calling that has been held at bay.

May we never walk in doubt and defeat again.

May we hold our head high as men among men and women among women.

May we stand as the kings and queens we were created to be.

May we see righteousness from our spirits spreading across the earth.

May we reconcile our spirit collectively upon a heavenly home.

May peace and blessings follow us.

May we labor for righteousness with the assurance that earth isn't home.

May we witness the presence of God as we awake each morning.

May praise for others live upon the tip of our tongue.

May strife and division live amongst us no longer.

May we find patience for those…

May we find patience for those who are still waking.

May we hold space for the wounded who wound others.

May we correct in love and protect with wisdom.

May we set boundaries that honor dignity and keep peace.

May we forgive without forgetting the lesson.

May we choose mercy without abandoning accountability.

May we slow our anger and quicken our listening.

May we answer offense with truth that heals.

May we become stewards instead of owners.

May we plant where we once only purchased.

May we repair what we did not break,

and return what was taken as a sign of covenant.

May our hands learn craft again.

May our minds learn discipline again.

May our households learn order again.

May our calendars learn Sabbath again.

May our tables feed neighbors before strangers applaud us.

May our speech bless before it boasts.

May our plans serve before they scale.

May our profit never outrun our principles.

May the elders sit at the head of our councils.

May the children outgrow our ceilings.

May mothers be honored, fathers be restored,

and families be fortified against despair.

May we choose study over spectacle.

May we choose service over status.

May we choose community over convenience.

May we choose legacy over likes.

May we teach wealth as the power to lift others.

May we count our influence by the lives made whole.

May we measure success by the justice we advance

and the joy we preserve.

May we remember earth as an assignment, not a possession.

May we tend the soil though heaven is our home.

May we leave rivers cleaner, streets safer,

and stories truer than we found them.

May the scattered find their way by our light.

May the doubting borrow our faith until theirs returns.

May the fallen meet our arms before they meet our judgment.

May the lonely learn family in our midst.

May we bless every nation that blesses the image of God in us.

May we refuse every system that buys our silence.

May we speak when truth is costly,

and stand when standing shakes the room.

May our mornings begin with gratitude.

May our noon hours carry integrity.

May our nights confess and reset,

that tomorrow finds us readier than today.

May leaders lead as servants.

May teachers teach to liberate.

May artists create to heal.

May builders build to protect.

May our covenant outlive our names.

May our unity outlast our trials.

May our witness outshine our wounds.

May our hope outpace our history.

And if we grow weary,

may rest visit us without shame.

If we lose our way,

may love be the landmark that returns us.

So let this be our vow:

That we will be faithful with little and faithful with much,

that we will be rich in good works,

and wealthy in the things that cannot rust.

Amen.

The Covenant of Homecoming– Chapter 3

Who don't agree, may we come into harmony with everyone.

May we live and let live without passing judgment.

May those who seek virtue open their spiritual eyes.

May we learn the difference between the temporal and the eternal.

May we once again find ourselves standing on the side of right.

May we love one another without feeling guilty.

May we realize that love starts at home.

May we reconcile our grievances with one another.

May we share our blessings with the less fortunate.

May we remember that the world belongs to the Father and can't be owned.

May we now do good for goodness' sake.

May goodness and mercy follow in our wake.

May our parks, schools, and communities be free from drugs.

May we give back the guns and violence, and the graves and prisons that come with them.

May we see ourselves without man-made stigmas.

May we give back the spiritual voices that have entangled us.

May our songs and raps now bring good cheer.

May we shout our deliverance for the world to hear.

May we find our footing within the near future.

May we reunite again with our cultural home.

May God deliver us from the hands of the oppressor.

May we come into a land of our own.

May our children finally know the birthright of a place called home.

May we come to the conclusion that a connection to a land and people can have no real fruitful existence without God.

May God give us a land that belongs to us.

May we become stewards instead of consumers over the earth again.

May we once again become Mother Nature's friend.

May the spiritual storms we've endured stay with us.

May we never forget the hand we were dealt.

May we come to believe in God's spirit as wealth.

May we become and make genuine friends.

May we find partnership among our fellow man.

May we renew our vows to become better men and women.

May we endeavor to love again.

May we find God through the wonders of creation, conscience, Scripture, and neighbor.

May the rivers teach us patience, the mountains steadfastness, the stars perspective.

May the work of our hands become prayer, and the love in our hearts become policy.

May we bless the soil before we sow, and thank the harvest before we eat.

May we return first fruits to the hungry, and wisdom to the young.

May we build wells where there were walls, and bridges where there were wounds.

May our justice be clean—without bribe, without bias, without hurry to harm.

May our officers be guardians, not hunters; our courts, refuge, not snares.

May our laws protect the poor, uplift the righteous, and correct the proud.

May our music lift burdens instead of bodies.

May our stories heal memory instead of weaponizing it.

May our art open doors for those history closed.

May our speech be seasoned with grace.

May we trade rumor for reconciliation, noise for knowledge, heat for light.

May we learn to disagree without dishonor and to correct without contempt.

May our homes become small embassies of heaven—

tables open, floors swept, chairs added, candles lit.

May fathers return, mothers be strengthened, children be seen and safe.

May our scholars teach truth without fear, and our students study freedom with discipline.

May apprenticeships return, trades revive, and libraries overflow with us again.

May we master tools, not be mastered by them.

May we steward wealth that cannot rust—character, covenant, craft, community.

May our currencies be trust and time well given.

May our ledgers show generosity as profit.

May the scattered find routes home.

May passports and borders bow to kinship and calling.

May the diaspora dance in one rhythm though many lands.

May the elders who carried us see rest;

may the martyrs who bled for us be honored;

may the children who follow us go farther.

May we choose the long obedience when shortcuts tempt.

May we trade spectacle for service, and speed for substance.

May we be faithful when unseen and the same when seen.

May grief not harden us, nor blessing make us careless.

May failure become curriculum, and victory remain humble.

May repentance be swift, and repair be thorough.

31

May we be led by the Spirit, not by fear;

by vision, not by vanity;

by covenant, not by convenience.

May our promised land be first a promised people—

upright, unbought, unbroken in hope.

May the map in our hearts match the justice of our streets.

May we keep watch at dawn, keep kindness at noon, keep courage at dusk.

May peace go before us, goodness follow us, and mercy walk beside us.

And when the day is finished,

may our rest be clean, our conscience clear, our love intact—

a lamp in the window for all who still seek home.

Amen.

The Covenant of the Crown– Chapter 4

Creation, may we and our children explore the world as our habitation.

May we once again seek out the mysteries of life.

May we find joy while doing so instead of suspicion and strife.

May we find favor among other tribes upon the earth.

May we agree to disagree.

May we find favor in the eyes of God.

May we, as a collective nation, find peace under the moon and stars.

May we find marriage to our woman to be sacred again.

May we find favor from our Black women.

Let us regain her love and trust.

Let her forgive the mess we've become.

Let God restore her virtue again.

Let us once again find her as our best friend.

Let our queens rise to the top.

Let her once again show us the vision of how a queen sits at the top.

Let her know peace and joy once again.

Upon giving birth, let her know, dear God, that her children are now safe.

Let her know that we have her back.

Let her know that we now know that God entrusted us with that.

Let us Black man and Black woman sit bodily before the throne of the King.

Let us see ourselves as equals supreme.

Let us show our beautiful Black children what true love really means.

Let us love our Black women from head to toe.

Let us show the world once again the way that love and not lust goes.

Let us renew our vows to love again.

Let us Black men find the scent that only love can give.

Let us once again woo her in courtship.

Let us walk and hold hands as man and woman.

Let us be each other's blessings and promise.

Let each new day find our bond stronger.

Let her find her way back to her leading all women of the earth instead of them leading her.

Let her regain her footing as Mother Earth.

Let the trials she's endured lighten her way.

Let her enemies now become her footstools and handmaidens.

Let her sons and daughters pour forth from her womb.

Let her find peace once again in nurturing as she was created to do.

May her rest be guarded, her labor honored, her healing unhurried.

May every birth be sheltered, every mother attended, every child received in joy.

May fathers return in strength and gentleness.

May our vows be kept in daylight and in dark.

May our homes be free from fear, our words free from harm, our hands faithful to protect.

Let our courtship be holy again—

patient, truthful, generous, and clean.

Let fidelity be our language, and tenderness our custom.

May sons learn honor at their mother's table.

May daughters learn safety in their father's arms.

May uncles, brothers, elders stand as watchmen at the gates of our homes.

May we repent of neglect, betrayal, and pride.

May we repair with truth, counsel, prayer, and consistent action.

May apologies become agreements, and agreements become habits.

Let our queens be seated where decisions are made.

Let their wisdom instruct policy, their courage steady our steps,

their vision set the horizon for our cities and our schools.

May our music bless our women and teach our boys.

May our stories retire the script of harm

and crown the script of care, covenant, and joy.

May midwives and mentors rise in every neighborhood.

May cradles be many, funerals be few, and hospitals be just.

May food be medicine, and tables be altars of peace.

Let rings mean responsibility, not performance.

Let love be work we gladly do.

Let arguments end with understanding, and anger end before sundown.

May we outlaw violence in our homes and laughter-proof our rooms.

May patience be our reflex, and humility our armor.

May prosperity never purchase our silence when truth must speak.

Let us Black man and Black woman build together—

budgets that bless, calendars that protect,

rituals that keep the flame when feelings flicker.

May our daughters inherit freedom without fear.

May our sons inherit courage without cruelty.

May our children inherit names without shame and futures without ceilings.

Let aunties, grandmothers, and sisters be honored.

Let mentors, coaches, and pastors be accountable.

Let neighbors become kin, and kin become a nation.

May grief not visit us as often, and when it does,

may it find us woven together—arms linked, prayers rising,

meals shared, burdens halved.

May forgiveness be a bridge we keep open,

trust a garden we tend daily,

and joy the banner over our house.

And when the evening settles,

may she sleep in safety, he keep the watch in peace,

and our children dream of a world we are actively making true.

Amen.

The Covenant of Deliverance– Chapter 5

Children once again become her blessing and not her curse.

Let her spirit once again come to life within the twinkle of her eye.

Let the joy within her heart pour forth from her lips.

Let her new songs of freedom be heard all across the world.

Let freedom and the end of tyranny now come to all Black descendants.

Let the notion of God forsaking His people be put to rest.

Let the Lord come for His people at last.

Let the chosen children of Israel be redeemed at last.

Let God's Holy Spirit wash us clean.

Let Him purify us from all idolatry.

Let us kill all tricks of the lower nature of the flesh.

Finally, go let our alliance and allegiance be to God and no longer Pharaoh.

Let us look to God in everything we do.

Let our actions and speech be pleasing to Him.

Let us stand in agreement with the Word and voice of God.

Let us never again walk within our own authority.

Let God's kingdom reside within our hearts.

Let His will be done through us upon the earth, as it is in heaven.

Let us admit our mistakes and seek His forgiveness.

Let us support Black children around the world.

Come to life.

Let our fathers and mothers rebuild our nations.

Let us as a people give voice to the voiceless.

Let us become the neighbor we desire to see next door.

Let us come to the conclusion that we're our own worst enemy.

Let us acknowledge the fact that we fell for the tricks of the enemy.

Let us rejoice within the fact that we have a risen King.

Let us live as if we believe in the thing heard about life after death.

Let us choose now while living heaven over hell.

Let the esteem of our people become enough.

Let us seek favor from one another.

Let us forgive but not forget the slave master's deeds.

Let us take the spiritual shape of the earth leaders.

Let us revive one another as we take command.

Let us push off the residue of the spiritual chains of bondage.

Let us become united in purpose.

Let our scattered gifts assemble like a body made whole.

Let our councils speak with one voice and many tongues.

Let our repentance be evidenced by repair.

Let apologies become restitution, and promises become policy.

Let our ledgers show justice as a paid-in-full line.

Let our pulpits preach courage and our classrooms teach craft.

Let our courts honor truth, our streets honor life, our music honor dignity.

Let our scholars and builders draft the blueprints of a freer tomorrow.

Let fathers and mothers rebuild the gates.

Let sons and daughters learn the names of the gates they will keep.

Let aunties, uncles, elders be pillars that storms cannot move.

Let us choose covenant over convenience.

Let us choose discipline over spectacle.

Let us choose stewardship over consumption.

Let land return to our hands as trust, not trophy.

Let gardens replace deserts.

Let houses become havens, and blocks become brotherhoods.

Let our economies circulate like living water.

Let our businesses tithe to the neighborhood.

Let our inventions serve the least first.

Let us disarm the tongue of slander and the hand of violence.

Let we who once wounded become healers.

Let we who once wandered become waymakers.

Let our diaspora become a single drum heard across oceans.

Let passports not sever what purpose has joined.

Let trade, study, and prayer braid us back together.

Let the Book shape our conscience and the Spirit shape our steps.

Let fasting break yokes and generosity break cycles.

Let Sabbath return to our calendars and tenderness to our homes.

Let mentors multiply.

Let apprenticeships return.

Let libraries fill and prison yards empty.

Let our artists remember we are archivists of hope.

Let our storytellers rescue memory from misuse.

Let our raps and hymns carry medicine and marching orders.

Let us keep watch over the next generation.

Let screens not disciple more than saints do.

Let play be safe, study be sweet, and futures be possible.

Let us resist Pharaoh in every costume–policy, platform, or price tag.

Let us fear God, not empires.

Let us follow the cloud by day and the fire by night.

Let grief make us gentle, not hard.

Let blessing make us grateful, not proud.

Let delay make us patient, not doubtful.

Let our councils be transparent and our books be clean.

Let leaders be servants and power be accountable.

Let titles bow to truth.

Let us write wills, fund trusts, and guard inheritances.

Let surnames carry honor, not harm.

Let tomorrow be wealthier because today was wiser.

Let forgiveness guard the door and boundaries guard the house.

Let reconciliation be a road, not a rush.

Let safety be non-negotiable and love be non-violent.

Let our feet be fitted with preparation.

Let our hands be trained for building.

Let our hearts be trained for peace.

Let our mornings begin with gratitude,

our afternoons with service,

our evenings with examen and rest.

Let the King's law be written on our hearts:

to do justice, love mercy, and walk humbly.

Let heaven's will be our daily work until earth agrees.

So let this be sealed:

We are allied to God, not Pharaoh;

to covenant, not chains;

to unity, not convenience;

to truth, not trend.

We begin now.

And we do not stop.

The Covenant of the One Drum– Chapter 6

To the Creator for direction and purpose, let us not go down with the colonizer when he pays for his and her sins.

Let us get busy rebuilding again.

Let us find our focus within these signs of the times.

Let the time be now.

Let us take a time out from spending.

Let us take a time out from borrowing.

Let God bless the child that has his own.

Let us unite in taking care of our own.

Let us not forget that we're one in humanity.

Let us remember that no one should love us as much as we love our own people.

Let us love others as we love ourselves.

Let us not nurture and love another more than we love and nurture self.

Let us remember that charity starts at home.

Let us internalize the fact that you can't help anyone else when your suffering is at home.

Let our love for our people so overflow that we have that much more to give to the world.

Let us acknowledge our tribe as deserving.

Let us find our God-given unique identity.

Let us once again raise our children as world leaders.

Let our sons and daughters forgive our sins.

Let them find their way home again.

Let the bells and trumpets in heaven sound forth.

Let us find peace within the journey ahead.

Let our forefathers and mothers sigh in relief.

At long last, let the Black nations around the world move to the beat of one spiritual drummer.

Let us seek out across the world our foreign sisters and brothers.

Let us retrace the paths of the colonizers' ships.

Let us rejoice in the held-at-bay reunion we're soon to behold.

Let us fest at every festival as one family.

Let every port around the world open to us.

Let us find in each of us the love of Jehovah.

Let every language barrier known to man cease for us.

Let our spirit of overcomers become contagious.

Let us stand up now as one people.

Let us not look to the colonizer for his permission.

Let us realize that every tribe must see to their own.

Let us as a people raise our children from the womb until they're grown.

Let rites of passage return, so boys become men and girls become women with honor.

Let aunties and elders anoint their steps and name their gifts aloud.

Let our houses become academies of faith, finance, language, and law.

Let bedtime stories restore our history, and breakfast tables assign our purpose.

Let homework include service, and graduation include covenant.

Let us build councils that are clean, cooperatives that are fair, and credit unions that are ours.

Let land be held in trust and not in vanity.

Let titles secure families, and deeds secure futures.

Let our budgets tell the truth;

let our debts be snowed under by discipline;

let emergency funds become ordinary, and giving remain extraordinary.

Let trade routes braid the diaspora—book for book, skill for skill, seed for seed.

Let ports and platforms open to us through excellence, not begging.

Let weavers, coders, farmers, and filmmakers sit at one table.

Let our languages return to our tongues;

let we greet each other in the names our grandmothers prayed in;

let we learn the scripts that once wrote our freedom.

Let our media be medicine—

no lies for clicks, no violence for rhythm, no despair for style.

Let truth be profitable again.

Let our health be holy—clinics close to home, gardens within walking distance,

midwives and mentors at the ready,

water clean, air respected, and food prepared with love.

Let safety be mutual, not militarized.

Let harm be met with repair, not revenge.

Let courts be refuge, and officers be guardians.

Let us partner with the oppressed of every nation without losing ourselves.

Let we keep our name while shaking hands.

Let treaties be signed in daylight and honored at dusk.

Let the drum call us each morning—discipline at dawn, diligence at noon, devotion at night.

Let our calendars reflect our covenant.

Let apprenticeships multiply—electricians, nurses, teachers, machinists, stewards of code and soil.

Let idle hands find craft, and restless minds find mission.

Let the work of many make wealth for all.

Let our sanctuaries train builders, not spectators; servants, not stars.

Let sermons become strategies and choirs become care teams.

Let offerings become scholarships, clinics, and shelters.

Let us certify our leaders by character, competence, and accountability.

Let books be open, budgets be clear, and power be humble.

Let titles bow to truth.

Let the diaspora assemble its archives–birth records, land maps, oral histories, names recovered.

Let the lost be found on paper and in person.

Let we sign our story back into being.

Let us travel to one another for more than funerals.

Let festivals seal our fellowship, and pilgrimages renew our vow.

Let passports be stamps of unity, not symbols of exile.

Let the trumpets sound–not for war, but for work;

not for spectacle, but for harvest;

not for empire, but for home.

Let our forefathers and mothers rest their worried hands.

Let them see in us the answer to their prayers.

Let our children witness promises kept.

Let our spending pause until our savings speak.

Let our borrowing hush until our building sings.

Let God bless the child that has her own and shares it.

Let our love of our people overflow until the world is watered.

Let charity start at home and never stop at the door.

Let hospitality be our halo.

Let us stop asking permission to be whole.

Let us remember every tribe must tend its own garden.

Let us plant, prune, and protect until it overgrows despair.

Let the one drum steady our steps:

discipline, dignity, diligence, divinity.

Let every heartbeat keep the time.

So let it be written in our deeds, not just our words.

So let it be seen in our neighborhoods, not only our dreams.

So let it be sealed in our children's names and our elders' peace.

We begin now.

And we do not stop.

Exodus from the American Dream– Chapter 7

Let those who have shared their union with another tribe continue there properly.

Let us turn a blind eye to the color of one's skin because Black love and expression comes in many shades.

Let all nations and tribes around the world join us in God's love as we lead the way.

Let the lie of racism complete its course.

Let us now realize that the God of the Heavens is the one who grants freedom.

Let us internalize that idolatry is its own prison.

Let us remember our forefathers and what our tired worldly experience is.

Let us stop chasing currency as a form of success.

Let us awaken out of the materialism fantasy, the here and now mentality, over delayed gratification.

Let us take theory/conjecture and God's opinions off our bargaining table.

Let us denounce the theory of measuring time or greatness solely by material accumulation.

Let us awaken as a people out of abortion as an epidemic.

Let us rethink the lie that children are curses instead of blessings.

Let us stop putting careers over our natural mission and obligations toward creation.

Let us give back the lie that for career, fame, fortune, and worldly success that our seeds must be flushed down the abortion clinics, drains, and sewers.

Let us be the moral leaders we were created to be.

Let the great experiment of the American Dream fade from the hearts of our people.

Let our passions and imaginations flow forth from our own wealth.

From wealth's sake alone does not equal security.

Let us understand that wealth must be used to direct the world's energy.

Let us come to the conclusion that resources are only provisions.

Let our materialism little boy and girl mentality see how full grown.

Let us learn how worlds acknowledge past and present.

Let the secrets of the world become open to us.

Let the influencers, wizards, and enforcers of darkness become our footstools.

Let us once again seek righteousness first.

Let us see God as Alpha and Omega.

Let us understand what the elite around the world do not mind – the accumulation of wealth as long as we don't know how to use wealth to change our outcome.

Let us awaken to our call of duty.

Let us become functional and directional from this day forward.

I pray we believe our own eyes and ears concerning our flight.

I pray that we believe that Donald Trump is proof that America is a corporation.

I pray that we understand that our names are America's stocks and bonds.

I pray that we are prepared if America is sold down the line.

I pray we come together around the world before America is replaced within a world collective banking system.

I pray today that we awaken.

I pray we awaken out of the spirit of the American Dream.

I pray this prayer with full knowledge that Africa's descendants have suffered the most throughout the course of history.

Entrapment of Lady Liberty's citizens, I pray we see past slavery, the Civil War and Reconstruction, and into the hearts and minds of Lady Liberty's leading men and women.

I pray we take into account her empty and broken promises.

I pray that we see that the Constitution of the United States of America is nothing more than a contract to entrap her citizens.

I pray we see through Lady Liberty's glutted woman's agreement.

I pray that we see that her citizen's lives are still up for sale.

I pray that we look to God and not a statue for virtue from now on.

I pray that we ask: Did Lady Liberty really serve her people or did we serve her?

I pray that we're her blindfold and spiritually undress her.

I pray that we see through the lies of her false democracy.

I pray that we see that for us liberty and freedom were both dreams and ideas given to our people.

I pray that we see that the will of the people was misused.

I pray that Lady Liberty fulfilled her own selfish deeds.

I pray we see her as robbed for what she is.

Whether Black, brown, white, yellow man or woman around the world, I pray that we see her as the seductress of the world.

I pray that we see her as the spirit of Apple and sinful pleasures of the world.

I pray that we see how she used us, her blind sheep, as pawns around the world.

I pray that we see that no other nation has displayed its sins as openly as Lady Liberty has into the rest of the world.

I pray that we see the biting of the Big Apple, referencing its sinful unimaginable pleasures as the reference to the Biblical connotation it is.

I pray we look through this lens when we see the United States.

Black America is in.

I pray we see clearly the mystique of her duplicity.

I pray we now understand the meaning and significance of lost sheep.

I pray that we internalize our state of spiritual emergency.

I pray that we turn to the Good Shepherd, our spiritual ancestor Jesus Christ, to guide us out of these old sinful belief systems.

I pray, as Black men and Black women, that we encircle elderly and children.

I pray that we turn away from the falsehood of belief that we must love the colonizer and their children before we serve, love, and protect our own.

I pray that we reject her scholars and return back to our God-given common sense.

I pray that we as a people heal quickly from the many wounds inflicted by her manufactured divisions.

Church Without Walls–Chapter 8

I pray that our spiritual light shines brighter now that we've tuned into the reality of our daily lives.

I pray that we realize that Lady Liberty's already woke culture has been pulling our puppet strings.

I pray that we denounce the Republican and Democratic political parties and for sale the American dream.

I pray that we no longer live in fear of other nations or people around the world.

I pray that we stop begging our colonizer for scraps off of his table.

I pray that we stand as one in prayer, as one in voice, as one as those of other nations who welcome our liberation.

I pray that we know beyond a shadow of doubt that we've been chosen by the Creator.

I pray that we realize that God's spirit that's within us is ready, willing, and able.

I pray that Black leaders in science, mathematics, agriculture, medicine, business, economics, and public speaking, and our philanthropists come around us as a nation.

I pray that we immediately cease any exploitation of our children.

I pray that we stop selling the colonizer's clothes, toys, and trinkets that have kept his children in overseer positions.

I pray that we invest in our own businesses.

I pray that we take our demands back to the head of America's leading corporations and age-old institutions.

I pray that we seek reparations.

I pray that we don't just demand it, but we demand the immediate relief of Mother Africa's debt.

I pray that we stop giving any nation involved with slavery and unrepentant absolution.

I pray that we globally see and envision life beyond the North American shores alone.

I pray that we never believe that man and not God can lead our ways.

I pray that we give back the colonizer's ways.

I pray that we return to a place of humbleness and grace.

I pray that our people are freed from the prisons around the world.

I pray that these prayers are answered by the God of Heaven.

I pray that we take on the newness of spiritual identity.

I pray we no longer feel the need to compete.

I pray we come to understand that the colonizer invented prisons and not our descendants.

I pray that Lady Liberty pays for her role in the crack epidemic.

I pray that the world comes to understand through realization that while they were watching the war on drugs from the safety of television, our communities were being overtaken.

I pray that our past sins meet with God's forgiveness.

I pray that our Black family that covers the earth like the beaches, multitudes of sand, now stands with the Son of Man.

I pray this prayer in Jesus' mighty holy name.

I pray that we become the living.

Church of our risen King,

I pray that we become the church as righteous individuals.

I pray that we realize that salvation hasn't been offered to the world in any other name.

…that we no longer feel the need to compete against one another.

I pray America pays for her role in the crack epidemic.

I pray that the world understands and comes to realize that while they were watching the war on drugs from the safety of their own homes, our communities were inside and out being overtaken.

I pray that our past sins meet with God's forgiveness.

I pray that we pray together as one family, that the earth like the beaches, multitudes of sand, stays together in unison with the Son of Man.

I pray in King Jesus' name.

I pray that we realize that America misused the church of our risen King Jesus.

I pray that we realize that salvation is promised through God's only begotten Son, Jesus Christ.

I pray that we now see the living Son of God that the truth has sent.

I pray that we see the need for a good shepherd in every event.

I pray we see the real shepherd that Martin Luther King Jr. spent his life telling us about, a prayer that goes beyond the things of the past.

I pray that none of us hold our breath when it comes to past.

I pray that we find peace inside our souls.

I pray that as a people we move into a higher power to stand upon the good.

I pray that we place our faith and trust to our elders in trust once more.

I pray that sinners stop telling the world the lie that Jehovah God cursed them, when every daily earned son provided the avenue.

I pray we stop looking to be the greatest of all time, when such pride and vanity originates from a lie.

I pray we learn to just be the greatest in time.

I pray we stop trying to conquer the world between dust till dawn.

I pray we return to be led and guided with God's Holy Spirit.

I pray we don't put off until tomorrow what can be done today.

I pray that the spirit of guilt is broken over all Black humanity.

I pray upon the earth as I write these words that the generations have yet to come may not feel lost because we put our tribe first.

I pray that we as a people become the body of Christ.

I pray that we become the church as righteous individuals.

I pray that our homes become houses of God as a family unit.

I pray that we no longer accept money as preachers of God's word.

I pray we push the gift of the gospel like little engines that could.

I pray we come to the realization that the church is the body of Christ.

I pray we effect change when injustice is seen, and not just…

...preach or speak about it.

I pray then as the church of Jesus Christ upon the earth we unite as freedom fighters.

I pray that the old ways of doing things pass away.

I pray that we as a people stop looking for the God that must be paid on Sunday to save our people.

I pray that we come out of the so-called church buildings and enter the streets.

I pray you know that the Lord's Final Supper will be filled only with the people He finds in the streets.

I pray that false prophets stop preaching for money.

I pray that everyone of us becomes satisfied with what we have worked for in life.

I pray that we stop trying to be perfect and wise in our own eyes.

I pray we accept the duality of our spiritual and physical makeup—our shortcomings and strengths.

I pray that we walk and talk with common sense.

I pray that creation all around us lights our way.

I pray that from the east as we did we know that our individual life came from the union of one man and one woman.

I pray we answer we know and lived as if we knew.

I pray that we give back the illusions and many ancestral beliefs about men and women.

I pray we give back God our imaginations.

I pray we heal when our spirits are cleansed.

I pray we're reborn in the baptism of spiritual fire.

I pray that God be the truth and every man a liar.

I pray that if we see it spoken, it will come to pass.

I pray we who put God's word on our heart and cross let God put His word on heaven and earth both passing.

I pray that we drop the titles and falsehoods of pimps, gangsters, crips, bloods, playas and macks back.

I pray that we come into our beings by the way of spiritual creatures living through physical conditions only.

I pray that we once again find value in brotherhood, fatherhood, motherhood, and friendships.

I pray that we learn that violence dœsn't solve our problems but protects us and our family from harm or imminent death.

I pray that we forgive the person who has trespassed against us.

I pray that we adopt a prisoner until they are free, and visit them regardless of why they are incarcerated if they have no support system.

I pray that we allow those who support our rebuilding of our nation to stand with us.

I pray that we use kindness and thanksgiving as our show of esteem and appreciation.

I pray that we honor our bonds of friendship that support our endeavor that we've made along the way.

I pray that we learn to stop and appreciate life itself.

I pray that we see goodness within ourselves before we see it in...

Church Unbound, Nation Restored– Chapter 9

I pray that Black becomes beautiful once again regardless of the many shades of color we come in.

I pray we turn away from the hypocrisy that the corporate church has given us of judging others.

I pray that we each bear our own cross along this journey.

I pray we seek forgiveness as individuals through repentance.

I pray we understand that the worship of God must come through a spirit of truth.

I pray we realize that then and only then can His work penetrate us.

I pray we see the trap of organized man-made forms of religion.

I pray that we never again enter their prisons–religious prisons.

I pray that we let love from now on become our light.

I pray we put our babies to go to bed full each night.

I pray that we stand up to the tyrants who have paved the way for bigotry and hate.

I pray we see God through His only begotten Son as we battle against Satan.

I pray we realize that our kingdom is here.

I pray the Kingdom of God we hold so dear.

I pray we walk in spiritual victory and never again within defeat.

I pray we see the dawning of Christ's Kingdom.

I pray we never compromise our morals for poor status or for money.

I pray we share our wealth with those of us less fortunate in their time of need.

I pray someone picks up our prayer line and continues this hymn.

I pray our Black anchors and producers bring life to their audience and viewers.

I pray that our radio announcers clean up their acts.

I pray that God's Spirit convicts them and frees them from the conviction of sin.

I pray we learn that the men and women thrown in prison cells are not the only people with convictions of sin.

I pray the real truth of the gospel reaches you as you're reading this.

I pray that we become free in Christ.

I pray we not only believe in the death, burial, and resurrection of Jesus Christ, but that we understand the spiritual power displayed from on high.

I pray we acknowledge the power displayed over death and hell.

I pray we choose this day to serve the Creator.

I pray that we learn that righteousness pays as well as sin.

I pray we learn to hustle righteousness and grind until we shine in spiritual form.

I pray we look to heaven for our treasure.

I pray that we keep greed out of the way as we steward the earth's riches.

I pray we acknowledge that our time on earth is for a season.

We see others as spiritual creatures.

I pray we wake up refreshed and full of hope.

I pray we learn better ways to engage life's pressure other than alcohol and drugs.

I pray we stop calling ourselves goons and goblins.

I pray we take our stand against being ruled by evil.

I pray we storm the orphanages and youth centers across America in search of our children.

I pray that we turn no stranger in need away.

I pray that we heal our own wounds first, before we take on the burden of others.

I pray that we slight no fellow man as we endeavor to heal with him.

I pray we never meet a stranger to be perfectly honest.

I pray that our brothers and sisters from other mothers sincerely join us.

I pray, I pray, I pray, O God that as we come together across the world God protects us from the spirit of hate.

I pray these prayers in Jesus' name, releasing God's power across our journey by sight unseen.

I pray our enemies become our footstool as the Word proclaimed.

I pray we rise quickly, effortlessly, and swiftly to the head of the race.

I pray we don't see life and death as a game to be played.

I pray death is defeated in the hearts and minds of each one of us.

I pray we find life in the action that keeps on giving.

I pray we remember that life and death is still in the power of the tongue that God gave us.

I pray that we seek the name above all names.

I pray that we tune in to our spiritual airwaves.

I pray that we learn to read the signs of the times.

I pray that we know that evil, sin, and wickedness are all systems against God that are running out of time.

I pray that the children of Israel scattered all are to be endowed in God's Holy Spirit as we are one unite.

I pray that we become the spiritual nation God's covenant conditioned.

I pray that the different colors of our skin become our greatest assets instead of differences.

I pray that the tower of Babel that separated our tongues finds us in spirit as one.

73

I pray that the first who became last all over the world become first at the continued reading of my words.

I pray our children show the spiritual fruitage of our transformation.

I pray that we stop claiming streets, blocks, and city's and claim the world as our habitation.

I pray that we come out of the block of the Judas across society.

I pray that our ancestors' advances live on through each and every one of us unselfishly.

I pray that God's will flows through you and me.

I pray that we become the change God called us to...

I pray we live, sleep, and breathe this prayer night and day.

I pray we never again need reason to believe.

I pray that we press forth into the light of day.

I pray we no longer listen to the plans America has for us.

I pray we now know that our God in Heaven is the best of planners.

I pray to the heavens and skies above to hear our cry of love.

I pray we cry out as one across the world.

I pray that Pharaoh hardens his heart so his fall will come quickly.

I pray that we expose all the darkness we've kept secret, dragging the evil of men into the light.

I pray that we confess our sins instead of hiding in darkness like a coward.

I pray we give back the prisons, early graves, and our mothers' broken hearts by giving back true belief in our God.

I pray we solve our problems, not with drugs, but with one another.

I pray that we give back the Black community's part in the running sex trafficking and evil nature of living and thinking.

I pray for our sons and daughters, sisters and brothers, and fathers and mothers' health and growth in spirit.

I pray that we honor in deed and word our past descendants.

I pray that we are not in new spiritual prisons.

I pray that we become one with God's new spiritual systems.

I pray that we become the light for others to follow.

I pray we fix our nations drinking water.

I pray we fix our dogs of greed who have enslaved the truth in our homes.

I pray we understand the need to possess the land.

I pray that we realize why our souls have not found rest.

I pray that we know that every Black must have a land of their own.

I pray that we assure our Black children of the safety of our own in our borders.

I pray that we police our own.

I pray that we no longer allow the myth of another race ruling over our people.

I pray that we crush racism's dissemination.

I pray that earth as it is in Heaven finds God's worship permeating more and more each new day.

I pray that we as a people worldwide lift our voices up to Heaven as one and sing a song of freedom from op-pression.

I pray that all the little Black children of the earth have plenty of vegetables.

I pray that they have enough food to eat.

I pray that we as a people and nation see to hunger's defeat.

I pray that we as a people stop consuming so much of the animal kingdom's meat.

I pray that we stop listening to man and start listening to the Son of Man as to who we be as a chosen race of people.

I pray we realize that as a race our time of leadership has come.

I pray we comprehend that with said leadership comes…

From Pews to Streets–Chapter 10

I pray we understand the reason for the appeal of our Creator's spirit to take over.

I pray we step into our role under God's system of righteous leadership upon the earth, full of spirit.

I pray we honor said commitment within our daily interactions.

I pray we unite as one under the Spirit of God and never again break apart into factions.

I pray that we from this day forward find serving God our only satisfaction.

I pray we as a people grow daily in boldness.

I pray that we storm the doors of unrighteousness wherever we find its principle and stronghold.

I pray that God becomes our president, governor, mayor, city councilman, and friend.

I pray we seek the Kingdom of Heaven and all its righteousness.

I pray we never again be lured into deals of mere men.

I pray we awaken out of the dream of misbelieving what God's Kingdom is, based upon us being perfect.

I pray we realize that God's Kingdom is based on His choice and our choice meeting up.

I pray that the realization that God's Kingdom is not yet being perfect, but about you having the trust through relationship to be led.

I pray your steady love spirit feed.

I pray that you know that mankind does not live by bread alone, but by every word that proceeds out of the mouth of God.

My hope is that you and I both were taught what to do and what not to do by the words of our parents, elders, and souls lived by the Word of God.

My hope is that we know that our time of reconciliation with our Creator is now upon us.

My hope is that we realize that the judging of the world by our Lord Jesus Christ is upon us as well.

My hope is that we know now that Santa Claus isn't the one we should have put our hope up against.

My hope is that we as a Black nation never celebrate with Santa again, or the Easter Bunny, or the Tooth Fairy.

My hope is that we only celebrate with the risen being Himself–Christ Jesus.

My hope is that my people is not in vain.

My hope is that we all as a nation become the spiritual glue the world needs.

My hope is that we realize that our fall from grace many moons ago stemmed from disobedience.

My hope is that we know that our hardships came by way of bringing us, the chosen children of our Creator, to full repentance.

My hope is that we internalize our reason for being allowed to go through the fires.

My hope is that we understand that others have not as a nation, thus for us been purified.

My hope is that we unite as one when God pulls from out each individual twelve tribes.

My hope is that we understand clearer now the bridge built back to Jehovah God through His only begotten Son's death, burial, and resurrection sacrifice.

My hope is that we now understand the power of redemption through the redeemer Jesus Christ.

I hope we acknowledge the path we must steadfastly take going ahead.

I hope you realize the King of all kings and Lord of all lords is alive and not dead.

I hope we rejoice as we walk boldly into the days ahead.

I hope you know that as Satan is defeated, Christ rose from death, so physical death has no sting.

I hope you know that the world has always anticipated this day.

I hope you know that your forgiving spirit and the willingness to call another race your brother and sister is the reason and only reason the God of pure love is sending us forth as first as change agents upon the earth.

I hope you know that we are the examples of what forgiveness looks like for other nations.

I hope you know that other nations are stiff, stiff-necked even though they say they ain't.

I hope you know that just as you were taken into slavery and your world came crashing down into spiritual darkness, so will others as you rise with God's favor.

I hope you know that as long as God is for you no one can stand against you.

I hope you know that those long-crushed bones from the slave trade found and reported back.

I hope you know that slavery didn't happen by chance, nor were you ever thought of as barbaric.

I hope you know that you have always been dominated as a noble people.

I hope you know that England was not the first nation to have a queen as head of state but the last.

I hope you know that your history has taught the world in the ways of culture and far exceeds these other nations' brief rulership periods.

I hope our mothers know that our children will never be taken into the custody of rulership by another nation.

I hope that they know that if they try civility will be broken.

I hope that other nations know that our children will never again be taken out of our homes and taken into their custody in any form.

I hope that this is our wake-up call as a nation to get on with the job of loving even through tough love our own.

I hope other nations realize that Black men and women have lived with the slave tactics or our children's mentality since we arrived here.

I hope that the ugly practice of meddling into the affairs of our households quiets within his dominion spirit.

I hope that He becomes his own nation's president, governor, and mayor and that they're practical or spiritually doing business.

I hope that when my nation reads these words they holla because I…

I need a witness.

I hope that all nations benefit from reading this.

I hope that all nations know that we love them.

I hope that other nations find pride in righteousness and not culture or color of skin.

I hope that our Black nation around the world follows Christ's description of love when it comes to our fellow man.

I hope that we understand the power of righteousness, and we never let the power within evilness.

I hope we see, understand, and from here on out, live the principle that if common sense dœsn't fail me, and crime or sin dœs not pay, then righteousness must.

I hope we realize that both unrighteousness and righteousness pays in equal effect.

I hope we choose righteousness.

I hope and pray we overcome as one.

I hope and pray all God's children come out of the shadows of spiritual darkness as one.

I hope that we see our homeland as our second home because God gave us both lands.

I hope China is the first nation to give Africa complete forgiveness and reparations.

I hope other nations do the same, and especially the nations who robbed her of her life force and vital energy by kidnapping her children.

I hope that our people of Africa welcome her sons and daughters from around the world home with open arms.

I hope that all Africa's descendants around the world understand that their strong is through.

I hope other nations of the world allow us safe passage out of their ports and borders as well as protection as we pass through.

I hope we never turn back from our work ahead just because the going is new.

I hope we find our journey liberating and exciting as well as secure.

I hope we tread lightly over the feelings of others as we allow God's spirit to separate us from all untruth.

I hope we give back all the evil spirits we've picked up over the last 400 years.

I hope we leave behind the falsehoods and lies we sold ourselves.

I hope we stand boldly and unflinchingly within the truth.

I hope we tell in faith in God as one tribe of African descendants wherever we reside and not in any man other than Christ Jesus.

I hope we call upon the heavens above to rescue our old, young, and future seeds.

I hope in the days ahead we restructure our very belief systems with the speed of lightning.

I hope we know we've been aware of this coming day since the first slave ship brought us in chains to this land.

I hope we know that our very ancestors prayed for this moment throughout the hardships heaped upon their very soul.

I hope we see our ancestors' freedom songs and old spirituals just like the Bible tells us the first-century believers responded in hope through oppression and persecution.

I pray we see victory from now on within the eyes of our brothers and sisters instead of hate and suspicion.

I hope we take hold to God's calling as our great commission.

I hope we unite as a tribal family in love under God's umbrella.

I hope America finally sees herself through our eyes and repays her past oppression and sins against us as a people.

I hope she finally sees the lie and flaw in the laws of "separate but equal."

I hope we put our children out of her schools and into our school, then across the land.

I hope we turn our hearts back to our children as our reasonable sacrifice as elders and parents.

I hope we usher in the fastest transference of a people ever.

I hope that we honor our prior commitments in the form of keeping our jobs in the lineage.

I hope we never have to beg for bread again or sell our body parts again.

I hope we never buy another designer label that keeps us broke and in the economic rat race, as well as our oppression locked upon us.

I hope we see freedom upon us after five hundred years of hell.

I hope you know that as righteous men and women, brothers and sisters can now be legally, morally, and spiritually set free from prisons and jails.

I hope you know that we were taken into slavery to subvert prophecy and to kill, steal, and destroy our legacy.

I hope you know that the hatred toward us is because of God's Spirit within us.

I hope you know that the one percent blood rule that this nation still uses to identify us has nothing to do with skin color but has everything to do with the oppression of our spirit.

I hope you know that Satan is recognized by his attitudes and spiritual devices so loud within when you see him in the heart and mind of mankind.

I hope we see outside the lies and sheepfolds that man has created for us.

My hope is that we focus our efforts from here on out as intelligent spiritual beings.

My hope is that we honor one another and the position God has given each of us.

I hope that we play our assigned roles along the way.

I hope that we use our talents to care for one another in community.

From Culture to Kingdom–Chapter 11

I hope we esteem our children and all children of humanity.

I hope we seek reality over the make believe.

I hope we become the salt of the earth in which it finds itself in desperate need.

I hope we turn to one another in our mind's eye core belief.

I hope we reach for one another as a single tribe and sheepfold of humanity.

I hope we look to God and the goodness of God inside of self.

I hope we endeavor to give one another as a collective nation our very best.

I hope we decide to build up our own.

I hope we love other nations and tribes as we love our own.

I hope we stay ahead of greed, vanity, and the pride of life.

I hope we never seek personal pleasure over the best for the tribe.

I hope my prayer reaches from me to you.

I hope it sincerely inspires you.

I hope you know that relationships are the foundations to success.

I hope you know that relationships are just how one thing relates to another.

I hope you learn as a people that in order to have good or great relations with people, places, or things we must first adequately identify the makeup and need.

For knowing the makeup of someone or their beliefs, we can determine quickly if outside influences affect the way they relate.

May we relate with love by using clarity.

May we see our influences as relevant.

May we move through life seeking and acquiring knowledge from God and apply it responsibly.

May we understand the old age wisdom that every human being plays a larger role in relationship to all things.

May we conceptualize that no one escapes responsibility.

Our Afro-Centric nation around the world become second nature.

Let us realize that we're all beholden to one another and that no one is lesser as a contribution or greater.

Let us begin the long journey back to being one with all things.

Let us peer into the wisdom of such belief and the harmony in which it inevitably brings.

May we as a Godly people walk in the spirit of our righteous God Jehovah only.

May we come away from the colonizers' belief that mankind was meant to own anything.

May we come away from being slaves to creation over the Creator.

I hope we see this day how the enslavement of man is done.

Let us be freed through the lost lure of the so-called finer things.

My prayer is that we see the war between culture versus society.

I pray we see the micro and macro difference between the two.

My hope is that we rethink our culture and uplift its effects upon society as a whole and vice versa.

Has our culture become our way of life—whether right or wrong—over the society in which we're part of?

Is it possible to infringe one's culture on society?

Do society's end cultures co-exist or clash?

What rules govern culture and society's?

Dœs society govern culture?

Do resources govern cultures and society's?

Do society's govern resources?

Do cultures govern resources?

Are society's made up of bosses?

Are cultures workers and consumers only?

Do society's uphold or tear down the culture's infrastructure?

Do cultures tear down society's infrastructures?

Do society's set the bar or lower it?

What is religion and why is there so much unknown mystery when someone asks the question. Does religion and culture mix? What role does religion play in the way society's are formed, if any?

As we understand religion, does the greater good of a culture or society throw religion out the window?

Does one small the effectiveness of the other?

Are cultures mini-society's enlarged?

Does culture mean the nurturing of a cult?

Do society's and cultures depend on one another?

Do I buy into those systems that come with their own beliefs, and if so at what cost?

My prayer for us is that we become the head, independent thinkers, and stop being the tail.

My prayer is that we wait on no man to lead us.

Our hope lies with a spiritual path alone.

Our hope should be centered on not what man has gotten right or wrong, but on our journey forward.

Our hope comes as an extension of our greater love.

The love we've given everyone else in spite of the world's abuse heaped upon us the world over.

Our legacy from this universal joining of our ancestors' offspring will grow and live on.

For our greatest gifts from now on must all stem from love.

Let us begin with the love of our own.

Let us not be silenced or shouted down through weaponized forms of division.

I believe that our voices today deserve to be heard.

Let the world take notice today because this day our declaration has been served.

I believe our children's voices being heard depend on our contributions going forward.

I believe that what we do today will speak into our future seeds tomorrow.

I hope we put sorrow to bed and may she pass away from our lives.

I pray we realize as spiritual beings that our very lives are ones of expression.

I pray we teach our children the art of creative, righteous expression.

I pray we choose death in this world from now on over being silenced by a man as our oppressor.

I pray we go back to our tribe's expression of certain things being unheard of or unnatural for our people.

Let's give the fruits of sin and the labor within back to the colonizer.

I pray we stop the physical forms of acting out just to be heard or get attention.

I pray we give back sexual perversion that has become permissive.

I pray that we know right from wrong in many ways just by watching creation.

I pray that we put our thoughts in order on a daily basis.

I pray that Jehovah restores us back to sanity after our five-hundred-year sojourn in the land of wickedness paraded as the light.

I pray we see the tongue of the enemy over the bright blinding lights that surround them.

I pray that all believers of truth know that truth stands alone and is in no need of accompanying bands or orchestras.

I pray we know there's no buts behind the acts we commit.

I pray we know the difference between forgiveness and one reaping what they have sown.

I pray we have sense enough to take the advice of those who say they forgive but still vote on the death penalty.

I hope and pray in making myself understood to those who don't take me.

Spiritual Nationhood Rising–Chapter 12

My prayer is that my people unite all over the world in spirit versus physical origin upon the earth.

I pray that the scales of darkness fall completely off of our eyes.

I pray we realize that our voice is our greatest contribution to any society.

I hope our voices become our gifts to a righteous nation through our thought processes and communion with God in play.

I pray we analyze the spiritual world around us and internalize that it's up to us to bring forth the word from spirit as physical expressed change.

I pray our hopes and dreams on how to lead the world out of spiritual darkness now take center stage.

We too have those hopes and dreams for a better tomorrow for the world in which we bring forth our children as seeds.

I hope we see that life is our greatest contribution.

I pray we see the future of our tribe. From the individual birth of each and every future child.

May we all stop the genocide of self-hatred and the many forms we re-create it.

I pray we come to the light of our own individual uniqueness and wear it like our favorite suit, set of clothes, perfume, or cologne.

I pray we know God created man and woman and that's it, and that's all.

I pray we see ourselves and nation as special before we ever again ask the world's other nations to see in us what we should already see.

I pray we realize how we got in this mental depraved condition of inferiority.

I pray you know that the slaves' mind was being conditioned first and foremost during the hundreds of years of slavery.

I pray we know this day that the Lord Jesus has made, that no other nation sees the world as beautiful as we.

I pray we become living expressions of the world we want to see.

I pray we are no longer silent when others are busy deciding what's best for us and our future generations.

I pray we now take the lead in deciding not only our future, but the minute details of humanity others have to date been working out for you and me.

I pray we come to the realization that the nation and world in which we live have given us pre-packaged and pre-approved sheep gates to go through.

I hope we denounce the governing system that offers us pre-arranged sheep gates to grind our lives will through.

I hope we come to the forefront of reshaping society's.

I pray we stop going through life blinded by the false light of others peacefully and quietly.

I pray we rebel against the present system that not only swallows our will but sets traps along the way to ensnare us.

I hope we see and recognize the cages of our colonizers' system ensnaring our seeds.

I hope we learn to live life like we see the linkage between us and our future generations or progeny.

I pray we condemn this present system around the world that incorporates our will at birth into its impersonal system and machine that dœsn't see you and me as fellow human beings equally.

I hope we raise our voice, and spirit, as one to call dictators in the place of power over the future of our nation.

I pray at the writing of these words, as this new day dawns, that heaven records our spiritual assimilation. May the curse of our blood on humanity, documented in the one percent rule, become our spiritual united blessing.

May our thoughts on righteousness never again be barred from public speaking.

May we never be told again that we don't understand the issues involving and surrounding humanity, as if God didn't equip us to nurture our offspring from the fruits of the earth – from the cradle to the grave.

Let us turn our face to our elderly and our youth around the world.

Let us seek to be the unbroken chain of humanity around the world.

Let this present despair fall away.

May we forever more awake into a brighter new day come what may.

Let us see this present system of old fading away.

My prayer is that we envision a new world where we co-rule with the spirit world leaders.

I pray we no longer see our value through the eyes of another nation.

Let us aspire to uncover our spiritual treasures.

Let us find praise and admiration among our distinguished nation.

Let us serve one another, and by extension, the other nations around the world.

Let us become accustomed to using our God-given intelligence once again.

Let our ability to reason stand above everyone else.

Let our spiritual mind become the very seat of Jesus Christ.

Let us never again be the instrument used by Satan to be or become the world's problems.

Let us never again seek to solve our nation's problems through violence.

May we see peace and love only as we lay eyes upon one another.

May our ghetto pass extend to our own people and nation.

May we rethink what leadership really means.

Let our values and morals as we rethink leadership always be preceded by our spiritual compass.

May we re-set the stage of our thinking patterns.

I pray we re-seat the leadership table around the world.

May riches of material possession never cause us to lead under the spirit of greed.

I pray we become satisfied once again with the notion of just being righteous.

Let the catch-22 of seeking fame, fortune, and riches fall away.

May we beseech one another to look down on the spirit of possessions wherever we see or hear of the followings of the spirit of covetousness.

May we as a people across the world internalize that no treasure has ever left the earth since King Solomon's before or after.

I pray we never forsake the value of spiritual treasure or the hereafter.

I pray our words become our greatest asset once again.

I pray we stand on our word and our promises, as well as our spiritual commitments.

I pray we never again take sinful liberties or freedoms as our right.

I pray we change overnight and become successfully spiritually tailor-made.

I pray we halt God's righteousness being sold down the drain.

I pray that through dialogue we give each other spiritual depth and perception.

I pray our God becomes our secret agent and favorite weapon.

I pray all these things in King Jesus' name.

Let us realize that we are the world around us and the majority of the good we see.

Let us give back the world's falsehood that wisdom concerning humanity can be found in the institutions that man has created.

Let us, as one, dare to speak.

Let our thoughts originate from Jehovah God before we debate.

May we only live from here on out in the presence of reality.

May we execute our spiritual transition seamlessly.

Let us grab ahold of our mental, fixed faculties.

For change must come to me and my people, and it starts with me.

May we usurp the actors on the stage who have kept us audience in ideology of beliefs.

Let us as a people rise up in spirit and stand to our feet.

May our standing up and no longer sitting down in the back of the bus become our new anthem, cheer, and declaration.

After all, faith without works is dead.

Let life become our best teacher once again.

I pray we once again find the joy in living only.

I pray we are never again ruled by the spirit of accumulating things.

I pray that we find ourselves concerned with the business of living, for the truth of the matter is that all things matter right down to the earth's supply of water.

I pray that we understand that all creation is within their appointed place in time.

I pray that we reach hold of our destiny in this space in time.

The Covenant of Appointed Time– Chapter 13

I hope that we come to understand that time is always of the essence because every thing happens through its permissive portal or window.

My hope is that we now realize that there is purpose through all living creation, and nothing happens through randomness or random selection.

Life is intentional and directional, and all creation is subject to subjection.

I pray that we as a people see that life is goal-oriented, driven, and all we purposely do must be done with belief within it.

I pray we go about building not only the spirit of mankind but our earthly systems orchestrated along these goal-oriented lines.

In life one must decide: freedom or slave, life or death in the physical and spiritual.

I pray we waste no time.

I hope we use time as our bookkeeper, score clock, reminder, and enemy when not used wisely.

I pray we conceptualize that time waits on no one.

I pray we tune into our ingrained clocks that tell us by the ticking of time that we all have duties and a purpose – something here to do.

Life has a purpose unique to the individual, yet shared through community.

We have a will, a will to not only live, but to give through the gift of leaving something behind.

Let our greatest will manifest itself in our will to decide right from wrong and choose right.

Let our will become proactive.

May our will become present in each and every living moment.

Free the wills presence is so powerful that we never stop thinking, wondering, daydreaming, and questioning life.

I pray that we as a people never question the gift of life again, only how to live it right.

I pray that we allow our wills to be governed righteously, but not by man any longer.

I pray our will lines up with the natural flow of the universe.

I hope we come under the universal understanding that our will's life force is not subject to or governed by matter.

Let us understand that the will is not tied to or governed by the flesh of mankind.

May we come to experience our will as the active force, power center, seat of unseen ingredient of our spiritual makeup.

Our biological clocks and wills are two key spiritual components of our makeup.

Every breath drawn testifies to life.

Every creation gives its outward judgment through breath to life.

I pray we once come to our wisdom and knowledge that has been stolen and hidden from our ancestors' teachings.

I pray we realize that information is key.

I pray our will to unseat the present rulers of this world through righteous knowledge.

Gathered and shared over, rules our will to occupy this physical body.

We can all agree that mankind's physical life span is one of weakness, sorrow, suffering, and pain.

We experience bouts of joy, love, good health along the way, but it's done at the mental and spiritual inclusion of the world's greater suffering and pain.

I pray we as a people awaken out of the individual thought processes of self all over the world. For we know that death is ever present and evidenced by the young as well.

I pray that we no longer view life as a game to be played and that we turn our attention to the business of living in freedom from man-made divisions.

We are information gatherers from our sojourn upon the earth.

We seek, quest, endeavor, and find, and pass on what we've uncovered to future generations.

But we're more than worker bees and worker ants in our place upon the earth.

For we harvest spiritual knowledge also and pass on the information.

We're givers and takers of the seeds of words passed on.

We're journeymen and women using our collective experiences as the bridge that others will walk, lay, and build upon.

We not only harvest wheat, but information as seed.

The planting or uprooting of ideas in the minds and hearts of our species have dual impacts depending on the quality of the information.

I pray we know who we are this day as spiritual creators of creation.

We can all agree that our knowledge and wisdom passed on is our key to growth, survival, genuine wealth, health, happiness, peace, and prosperity.

We can all agree that the information we're armed with determines our course and journey.

We've been denied our history, and with it our very identity in God and relationship built over the years.

What was is still being done to us and at an accelerated rate I fear.

Can we agree that mankind is collectively part of our past generations?

Time, Will, and Holy Dominion—Chapter 14

Can we agree that mankind is collectively part of our past generations?

Can we agree that our roots, our makeups, our experiences, and the way we see and relate to the world—uniqueness right down to our DNA, passed through childbearing—are recorded as part of our nation's continuation?

If so, can we call our life's journeys anything less than gifts to future generations?

Isn't each life woven into the greater story of not only our nation, but the universe itself?

Every life arrives by the gift of one to another.

The universe records our individual stories and, by nature's decree, weaves them into a far larger tapestry for its own pre-destined purposes.

I pray we each, and then all together, search our souls.

I pray we give everything inside us to our nation's larger story.

I pray we give as our women and mothers have always given—love fueled completely from conception through birth and beyond.

I pray we, as fathers, learn to love by raising our seeds emotionally.

I pray we teach our children how to attach their hearts to their children.

I pray our sons and daughters become more than re-arranged schedules, borrowed expectations, or vessels for our unfulfilled dreams.

My hope is that we teach our children to love and laugh, to carry emotional strength, and to walk beside their children for as long as life allows.

After all, isn't a parent's love all-consuming before the child is even seen?

I believe slavery preconditioned too many Afro-centric men to detach from their children.

I believe hardship has clouded our vision of what it means to be a man.

Our ancestors did not arrive on slave ships with the roles of man and woman undefined; hardship impaired what was clear.

I believe my people have drifted from being a people.

We have lost the common thread of continuation.

We stand on the shoulders of those before us, yet as the world's largest consumer group we have become takers instead of givers.

I pray we reverse the curse.

I pray we reform society through medical breakthroughs, cleaner energy, and higher learning.

I pray we become givers of life that keeps on giving.

I pray we see how our history is too often capped at five to ten years of remembrance in our children's minds.

I pray we recognize the American Dream as the killer of a nation's tribal history.

Is it any wonder our youth search only city blocks and neighborhoods for their past?

Do we still record our people's contributions—or has our history shrunk to a month while a slow genocide plays out against our nation by us and by outsiders?

Where is our wisdom evidenced in the values we collectively display?

We know each nation sees the world through its own unique experience. Our material treasures remain on earth, but spiritual treasure lives on—so let us lead again in spiritual contribution.

I pray we become one with life's continuation and purpose—divine agenda.

Let the memories, prayers, love, sacrifices, dreams, and fulfilled visions become part of our being—and let us pass them on.

Let our very selves conform to service.

Let a spiritual compass guide us, our footprints set upon time's pattern as we give account to the universe and, by extension, to one another.

I pray we give life through service, erasing stigma and worthlessness.

Let us reject the rat race of men.

Our value is pre-recorded and predestined; we were made whole from birth.

Let no nation tax our wills or drain our life force again.

Let us focus on building our nation—here and abroad—mentally and spiritually.

Let us ensure our children's wills are never enslaved by another people unpurified as a whole.

Let us never again trust our children to another nation.

Let us rise, teach, reach, and nurture our own.

May our children's wills never again be assimilated into the will of another nation's forefathers.

Let fathers and mothers stand firm upon the mantle of parenthood.

Let us find our feet after centuries spent crawling after a colonizer's whims.

May we become a nation of independent thinkers, at one with reality and not fantasy.

Let us see things as they are.

Let common sense be our measure.

Let the evidence of concentrated exclusion move us toward independence from selfish movements.

Let hardship translate into spiritual progress, growth, and development—not into isolation from truth.

Progress of the spiritual kind is the accumulation of generational lessons.

Trial and error spring from chaos, disorder, and the lack of clear direction.

Let every trial become our stimulant—the fuse of our spiritual rebirth re-lit.

Let this prayer become building blocks for the next generation.

May our words be of life and not death.

May what we speak be recorded in the hearts and minds of our descendants.

Let our words become faith toward a life beyond earth.

Let our speech create spiritual life and a desire to live righteously upon it.

May we take responsibility for the unfolding of the next generations.

May our universal consciousness value the spiritual over the merely physical.

Let us remember who we are—the height of creation—and teach our offspring who they are as their first lesson.

We are the recorders of history and the keepers of time.

We have dominion over the earth; our greatest power resides in our spoken word and conscious thought, shared and passed on.

Everything on earth was created for human stewardship, yet we glorify creation while forgetting our own created purpose.

We are duality in motion.

No multitude of species records our spiritual passage.

So ask: who records us in time?

Let us teach our children that everything upon the planet was fashioned with humanity in the Creator's mind.

We eat of every tree and from every animal kingdom for physical nourishment, yet our spiritual being is not fed by such things.

And though creation was not made to consume us, we have become slaves to things made from it.

Let this knowledge point to our dominion—and to how far we have fallen in our approach to society.

We are born beings; no occupation can add to that essence.

May we occupy Godliness first.

Let our will seek the Kingdom of God—the right way humanity was designed to operate.

Let our allegiance be to God's way of seeing, the path our steps should follow.

Let the government of truth come to earth as in heaven.

Let us believe—if we believe in God—in the spirit world and in life beyond our physical universe.

May those who believe in life after death confess life above.

May those who hope in the hereafter walk as if they belong to the coming kingdom even now.

May our interactions reflect our beliefs with common reason and common sense.

May we see through the misapplied divide between "spirit" and "spirituality."

Let spirit outvote hypocrisy.

Let righteous living define our values.

Let us turn away from "spirituality" wielded to govern conscience by man-made laws that condemn rather than heal.

May we use spirit as guide—universal law and principle.

May we walk in dominion from this day forward.

Let us be one with God through the redeeming sacrifice of His only begotten Son.

Let us reason with mature, God-minded consciousness.

May this mindstate authenticate our spirits' value among the world's tribes and nations.

May we conclude that God gave a world that testifies to humanity's greatness—even as we struggle with love, peace, and goodness.

Technology has shrunk our world, placing the universe in our living rooms at a touch.

Our spoken word now travels farther through the art of communication.

What we need is the King of kings' systematic approach to government and governance—shared across the universe.

We are moving as a spiritual species past the point of no return—toward a worldview of servants rather than tyrants.

To serve is to honor all mankind and to bear witness to the order in which the universe thrives—the natural rhythm that grants us the best chance to live free of chemical and pharmaceutical chains.

I pray we give back the drug culture we have upheld and reinvented.

I pray we rediscover natural ways to unwind, to socialize, and to enjoy fellowship with one another again.

From False Lights to Living Truth–Chapter 15

I pray we finally see how a nation became a free market for drugs it does not grow, and how criminalization turned into a catch-22 that taxed the wounded.

I pray we name the evil at work, and recognize the cold-blooded pattern–genocide replayed and rebranded.

I pray we do not confuse today's trends with yesterday's war waged against our communities.

I pray we abandon hopelessness–the gateway to defeat.

I pray we fall in love with one another again, and learn to love ourselves as bearers of a singular, God-given identity.

I pray our joy returns to our faces, our laughter to our rooms, and our dancing to our streets.

I pray we keep the devil underfoot whenever he lifts his head.

I pray we live Spirit-fed and never deny the voice of God because men say intimacy with God cannot be had.

I pray we, as a nation, embrace the real supernatural and adapt to the spirit world's reality.

I pray we seek God's favor and stop looking to men as saviors.

I pray we shake off slavery's shackles and refuse the lies spoken in God's name.

I pray we see history through the eyes of the crack years, systemic racism, the courtroom and the gurney—and separate our fate from the systems that authored them.

I pray we advance and stop gazing backward at darkness; let the lies, treacheries, and false holidays fall away.

I pray we look past bombs and bravado into the wisdom of God.

I pray for release from prisons—brick, steel, and invisible.

I pray we find one another across the world.

I pray we unite our cause and expand our spiritual gifts.

I pray nations that love justice stand with us as we walk in truth.

I pray we become guardians and custodians of the Word wherever we travel.

I pray we stop believing we were forsaken; let hidden things be revealed, and secrets kept in darkness come to light.

I pray we move as one into all truth—and prepare for it.

I pray we forgive ourselves for our failures and begin again with clean hands.

I pray we codify protections so our children are not taken from our homes, and families remain whole.

I pray boldness rises from our awareness of a divine mandate.

I pray we leave dependency behind and remove our people from the shackles of incarceration by due petition and due process.

I pray restoration descends upon us—mind, body, and spirit.

I pray we recover our roots and move as one nation under a healing groove.

I pray artists and influencers lift the streets—

that Jay-Z and Beyoncé mobilize platforms,

that rappers, gospel singers, actors, and creators join one banner of peace and reconciliation.

I pray this becomes a family reunion, a final call to a people still living under occupation.

I pray we stop fruitless spending and start building—

buying shares, not status; gifts that compound, not clutter.

I pray we seed our children's accounts by seven,

and stop spending where love never returns.

I pray we flip the tables on greed,

choose patient investment over lotteries,

and do trench work—physical and spiritual—together.

I pray we trust the ancient wisdom of God more than the fashions of men.

I pray we remember the gospel is not the property of any empire.

I pray we honor our distinct spiritual design without shame,

and value the journey that forged us.

I pray we rebuild systems that make peace possible and prepare for trials with steady souls.

I pray we stand on the world's stage as heirs—not caricatures—

retiring labels that shrink us and restoring names that crown us.

I pray we pull back the veil on duplicity and move forward with hard truth in love.

I pray we keep our people first in our planning, embrace oneness of spirit, and follow no voice that is only speech.

I pray we stop waiting for a return when the command to act in righteousness is already given.

I pray we reject stardom, fill in the blanks, and become the change we keep asking for.

Service Over Spectacle– Chapter 16

I pray you know there is no higher calling than to serve humanity.

I pray you remember every deed is seen, every act recorded.

I pray you understand why we all need a Savior, and that life is a choice between right and wrong.

I pray we return to a divine standard of living.

I pray we embrace freedom from evil and denounce schemes that exploit.

I pray we stop, look around, and begin changing the ground beneath our feet.

I pray we envision a world where harm is healed and justice restores.

I pray we make this world better for all children.

I pray we tell the enemy of mankind: your lie ends here.

I pray we become change agents–beginning at home.

I pray we become the best our neighborhoods have ever seen.

I pray our sisters look left and right and see a sea of honorable men.

I pray we fall in love with love again—its taste sweet, its gaze free of suspicion.

I pray we awaken to leadership with love as our super-power.

I pray we ask leaders and pastors for a people-centered vision.

I pray we see a future free of tyrant leadership.

I pray peace on earth becomes our collective assignment.

I pray we gather as a tribe of conscience before blending with others.

I pray our wandering ends and our mending begins—hearts, minds, and homes.

I pray we remember: without vision, people perish.

I pray children arrive beneath vows kept and homes whole.

I pray we become the pattern of spiritual oneness others look to.

I pray we remember: we are the church, the classroom, the marketplace of good.

I pray we guard our inner story.

I pray our family tree stretches its arms around the world.

I pray we cherish our many dialects, cultures, foods, styles, habitats, and gifts.

I pray we honor a global kinship that spans seas like grains of sand.

I pray our priorities shift from performance to purpose.

I pray we leave the grind of empty status and remember we were born for greatness.

I pray we do not sell our birthright for applause.

I pray we leave consumerism for stewardship, spectatorship for building.

I pray our children come into the world as lenders, not borrowers.

I pray we sit at the head of the table—no longer fed by fables.

I pray we stop seeking approval from any empire.

I pray we return knockoff truths and stand in the Word made alive.

I pray we walk in a spirit of truth.

I pray we become keepers of our brothers and sisters.

I pray we sow only seeds of righteousness.

I pray we say plainly what things are and learn our whole history—not a month, but a mandate.

I pray we remember our women are called Mother Earth and our first home is called the Motherland.

I pray we piece the spiritual puzzle back together and draw strength from perseverance.

I pray we see beauty in every shade and wear our heritage with joy.

I pray we build ownership and enterprise.

I pray we seek the mind of Christ in every matter.

I pray we never again accept the lie that faith came to us last.

I pray we set the record straight about theft, debt, and the dignity of our people—

and aim our demands toward justice, not trinkets.

I pray we remember: we were a people before, during, and after oppression.

I pray we lead humanity toward a brighter day.

I pray we examine every authority and test every spirit.

I pray we learn that no one defines us but God.

I pray knowledge of self births love of self;

love of self births respect for self;

respect for self births respect for life.

I pray we drink from living water and feed on what truly gives life.

I pray we repent—a 180, not a 360.

I pray we let consequences teach without canceling mercy.

I pray we stop throwing stones at prisons and start removing ourselves from the pipeline.

I pray we choose plans and vision—two tools systems fear.

I pray we refuse the master-slave mindset wherever it hides.

I pray we breathe—deep and collective—and thank the Shepherd who values the one percent remnant and leaves the ninety-nine to find it.

I pray we see that even a remnant can redirect history.

I pray we remember: religion is not the cage; Christ is the door.

I pray we hear Revelation's warning to the seven churches and choose the path that is not rebuked.

I pray we believe in the One God sent and trust beyond man's credentials–

beyond banking and vanity, beyond systems that flatter and fail.

I pray we become followers of the Living Word, led by the High Priest, Redeemer, Way-Maker.

I pray we stop living by fallen promises and stand under promises that cannot fail.

Amen.

Renewing Our Bond with the Creator– Chapter 17

Let us each renew our covenant with the Creator.

Let us pour our will into the wisdom given about life after death, and make the coming days our determined best.

Let us refocus.

Let us turn from palm reading, astrology, and divination–not because they are powerless, but because they speak of creation and not the Creator.

Our Father needs no interpreter; the heavens already declare His glory.

We do not need magic to seek His favor or presence.

I pray we now believe our spirits need resurrection.

All born of man are born into sin; the commandments warn us because our fallen nature is capable of much.

I pray we turn from the world's lures that press us to conform.

I pray we are freed from stigmas stamped on our skin and bloodline at birth.

I pray barred paths open, and the way to our God-given goals is cleared.

I pray we never feel orphaned on this earth.

I pray we know the spiritual legacy of our national family tree.

I pray we reject the lie that we are merely workers; we are purpose-bearers, not payrolls.

I pray our callings are fulfilled while we live, not merely memorialized after we rest.

Let Christ Jesus be the vehicle by which we are delivered to the world.

Let true doors open before we ever wander into false ones.

Let us use God-given gifts, not superficial props.

Let us honor the inborn Spirit that leads us to co-create.

As we think, so we become.

Let us understand God's will entrusted to humanity and consent to be led.

No one can force our will; the enemy crafts conditions to make compromise sound sweet.

For centuries, here and in Mother Africa, others profited from our co-creative will.

Let us reclaim it—God-centered, peace-driven, for good will on earth.

The larger the believing, the greater the momentum.

Let us walk as spiritual beings moving through physical conditions.

We alone continually receive new information and re-evaluate.

We live in progression; our people are due to make landfall because the Source of discovery is always before us.

Trust God, not money.

To trust in money is to trust in man, for Cæsar prints it—but he dœs not create the earth's produce.

We are catching up and catching on; let God be our Source, and let resources follow the Creator, not the other way around.

A species that steadily improves has direction; we are headed somewhere.

Our duty is to help restore a fallen world.

We are connected to all things, seen and unseen.

We live not by bread and water alone; our species lives by the word—spoken, written, remembered, and passed on.

Truth or lie, risen word or fallen word—what we teach our children governs growth and decay.

We are not accidents of evolution; words are the torches that light or darken the path.

Guard what is said about who we are; our belief window is not for sale.

We can grow spiritually even as the material world hemorrhages under greed, pride, and vanity.

Knowledge—applied and shared—is how humanity evolves.

We have been last, and we will be first—Afro-centric sons and daughters across the world.

Will all turn? Time will tell.

But the real question is not "to be or not to be," it is: how can intelligent life fail to know itself spiritually?

Teachers of one or many, answer this: who do you say we are as human beings?

We named every creature and classified every kingdom, yet pretend amnesia about our own origin?

If knowledge was hidden, stolen, or dulled, then intelligence is our retrieval:

to collect, compare, reject, comprehend, and pass on a spiritual harvest.

We are travelers, retracing our steps toward highest destination.

We are already in space—look up; we are suspended in time for a brief span.

We gather knowledge and create from what we gather.

We are living pœtry, thought in motion, receivers discerning signal from noise.

See the spiritual death that comes from feeding on lies;

belief becomes a navigation system.

Do not sentence a soul with fallen names.

Life is not a fantasy—dreams visit us, but reality requires choice.

So let us foresee a Kingdom consistent with what we claim about life after death.

Let us seek the righteous path—personally and collectively.

Let us see ourselves as holy.

Let a Black nation rise in righteousness—men and women searching the mirror with courage.

Let this prayer root in every heart.

From now on, life and death will be read in our yes and our no.

I entrust you with this obligation: love God, love yourself, and love our nation—before presuming to love another.

www.ingramcontent.com/pod-product-compliance
Lightning Source LLC
Chambersburg PA
CBHW071515120626
46550CB00006B/2231